To MINE OWN
SELF BE TRUE

Tumultuous Journey, Poems Along the Way

J. G. Woodward

**Tumultuous Journey,
Poems Along the Way**

Invincible Publishing
1107 North Howard Street
Akron, Ohio 44310-1331
T: (330) 923-8405
F: (330) 940-3052
W: www.invinciblepublishing.ws
E: info@invinciblepublishing.ws
    orders@invinciblepublishing.ws

ISBN 978-0-9801214-0-7 Hardcover

Printed in the United States of America

Table of Contents

4

About the Author

J. G. Woodward was born and raised in Ohio. Her heritage is from her father, her hero, who came from Caracas, Venezuela, and died many years ago, and from her mother, who was born and raised in Richmond, Virginia, and was ever quick to recite her lineage to Edgar Allan Poe, General Robert E. Lee, and President George Washington.

Ms. Woodward obtained Bachelor's and Master's degrees from Kent State University. After graduation, she lived for many years in Charleston, South Carolina and Tampa, Florida, returning home some fifteen years later. Her lifetime career is as a Rehabilitation Counselor.

She now makes her home in Akron, Ohio, near her brothers and their families. She lives with her life partner and pets of varying degrees and temperaments!

Preface – Note to the Reader

My first poem was written at the age of sixteen and they have translated from my head to the page since that time. They spill from me as though I cannot get them down quickly enough. It is only due to the insistence of those around me that this collection has been produced for all to see.

My youth was spent in active alcoholism. Yet, I somehow managed to complete college and start a career. Arriving at the edge of demise, I found recovery and have not since had a drink, by the grace of a power greater than myself, for certain.

My mother was the first to believe in my talent, though our relationship was always strained. Having a gay daughter was a hardship as it was not a good vehicle for societal acceptance for her. She was ashamed of my sexual orientation but proud of the woman I am at the same time. In 2006, the rift in our relationship due to my sexuality finally made us estranged; I believed our relationship to be forever severed.

The poems in Tumultuous Journey, Poems Along the Way, were written in 2006 and 2007, the most difficult time of my life. It was a period that took me through heart wrenching despair, great efforts to maintain sobriety, and the throws of clinical depression. It ultimately ended in great joy and happiness, the place from which I write to you now.

I met my best friend and married her a year later. We had ten months together before she was diagnosed with breast cancer. She was a young woman and she fought hard for her life for three years, but lost. I remained her best friend and life partner, and I became her sole caregiver.

The emotional turmoil of watching the person I loved most in the world suffer and struggle was compounded by having to maintain my full time career and providing the majority of our financial support. Many reports were completed next to her hospital bed.

Being a gay woman, I had no civil rights that are so taken for granted by most. I did not have the privilege of placing my partner on my health insurance; I could not take leave under the Family Medical Leave Act, a United States Federal Law, in order to care for her, being guaranteed my job after her death. Having nothing to gain by sharing my plight with my employer, I chose not to do so, lest I draw the eye of scrutiny to my work, the only source of income in our home.

It was when my partner had only three weeks left to live that I finally told my employer of the events of my life over the prior three years. I requested personal leave from my employer to care for her full time. My employer was supportive and graciously granted me six weeks of personal leave but did not award me the twelve weeks that the federal government mandates to be given to married males and females in the same situation. I was grateful to my employer for what was given me.

My partner began taking Morphine three weeks before her death and the beautiful love that we had known for so many years turned to ugliness. With friends in the legal field and family now in the picture, the combination of drugs and influence resulted in her changing her will. She gave our home and her belongings to her family and told me I could sleep on the couch if I so wished; family members would be sleeping on the pull out sofa bed that had become my place of rest for the prior year due to her discomfort.

I returned to my childhood home to be near family and friends, to heal, leaving my home and everything behind. The legal battle needed to reclaim my life was not worth the cost to my emotional well-being; it was not worth the fight for one woman against the government that did not even recognize my marriage to begin with.

The blessing in all that passed was that upon returning home, my mother became my best friend, the sole person to know of the depth of my despair. She comforted me and was truly a mother to me while I struggled to harness my grief and while competing for a new job with my employer, some one thousand miles away from the position I left. I was fortunate that my employer found a position for me back at my home in Ohio.

The wedge that had divided my mother and I for a lifetime, my sexual orientation, dissolved. She proudly told all who asked of my sexuality and pledged her pride in me, whatever my sexual preference. Three months after I returned home to Ohio, my mother died suddenly and unexpectedly.

Grief has a funny way of catching you, whether you acknowledge it or not. Still, I survived, I stayed sober, and I kept my sanity.

This tangent of my journey is behind me now. My brothers and their families are a part of my life today and by the very grace and compassion of the universe, I have found love again.

This love is like no other; it makes me soar. I can't say that I would go through all of it again in order to find the love I now know, but most certainly, I am so very grateful to have found this, the greatest love of all.

May this book help you to heal and find peace,

J. G. Woodward

Acknowledgments

This collection is dedicated to my mother, Josephine, the first to recognize me as a poet and the first to encourage my words; to my father, Frank, my favorite person, from whom I learned integrity; and to the memory of Susan.

Gratitude and thanks go to Clare, the inspiration for transcription of a life's work; to Larry, for convincing me of the worth in so doing; to My Audrey, whose dedication and love have been the cement that binds me and the love that propels me; and to Dr. Bob S., Bill W., and H.P.

I have finally reached the age where the wisdom of my years outweighs the idiocy of my youth.

Ponder

Quandary: win or lose?

I sit in suspension,
    hovering on the edge of reality;
      fantasy allures me.

The various probable futures stretching
out in endless paths before me,
  calling,
    daring,
      futility in entertaining their existence.

Yet, I ponder.

Perhaps

Centeredness evades me,
  my thoughts always racing into the
  "what if's" and "but for's".

I close my eyes and the thoughts cease
  but the visions appear.

Dreams of hope and possibility,
  intrigue and fascination,
    loom before me,
      inspiring.

My eyes open and I sigh,
  knowing that what is before me is so very
  far away.

Thoughts return,
  accompanying me through the day,
    whispering,
      "...perhaps."

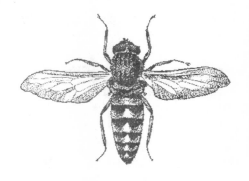

Parables

Consequences of distant past rear up to
dissuade me,
  tenacious their hold,
    deterring my intent.

Ghosts appear,
  reminding of the grip once held.

"Coward!", I cry,
  cursing their presence.

Resolute, I awaken,
  cautiously dressing in my daily armor,
    wielding a proverbial sword at my
    traitor past self.

Knighted, I dub myself,
  to take on the demons that dwell in the
caverns of the past.
    Damn them!

Victory in their taming I will attain;
  yet, never able to fully demolish or
  destroy their lifelong presence.

Parables.

Sentenced

How long is it that I should remain faithful
to a memory?

At what point would the reasonable forgive
herself for transgressions of the mind?

Solitude, my constant companion,

   introspection, my foe.

When the mind ceases, the pen resumes.

   Beckoning, challenging me to dare hide
the truth within,

     unrelenting,

      unerring.

Sentenced.

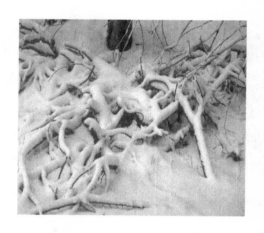

Crystallization

The veil of mystery that has shrouded my
recognition of your identity gently falls
away.

My view no longer murky,
  my vision clearing,
    you appear before me.

All that you are,
  the woman that is me,
    unfolds into destiny.

The path once obscured discloses its
intention.

At last I have more answers than
questions.

Crystallization.

Caution

One cannot maintain neutrality,

yet live life with passion.

Sides must be chosen,

opinions adhered to,

in order to feel deeply,

sensuously,

penetratingly.

Caution services no one but the cautious.

Perish

I sit in despair,

    attempting to see the higher value of it
    all.

Each day longer than the last;

    each turn of the path a twist in my heart;

      I whither slowly along the course.

But for newfound hope,

    surely I would perish.

Behold

I see your temptation to believe in an
accepting, non-persecuting God,

   a twinkle of hope that perhaps it exists
   for you.

The God of tradition,

   preached and imposed,

     still holds you.

The unconditional love of the power who
so long ago forgave you awaits,

   lingering,

     a faint image in the mist of imagination.

Behold.

Surrender

Love:
  colorless,
    genderless,
      boundless and blinding,
        yet, all seeing.

Draws you,
  daunts you,
    drives you to challenge your
    preconceptions of love's definitions.

Borderless,
  prideless,
    and often inconvenient,
      yet, promising.

Surrender.

Freedom

I flee from the prison of my everyday
existence,
  panting, screaming,
    the hold elastic, flexing,
      drawing me back to the pain.

Release me!

The pain eases as the distance increases.
  My soul wrenches free of the agony,
    bursting into sprint toward my future,
     calling me,
      awaiting me at destiny's gate.

Freedom.

Consulted

I sit in the center of the suspense of my
life,

    observing as the pieces move of their own
    volition,

       shifting,

        changing,

          varying in focal point.

If only I were consulted...

Foreshadowing

It seems silence is what provokes my
written word;
  unspoken,
    but not unfelt.

Dismissiveness!

The story unfolds;
  the path chronological,
    but not linear.

Music silences my restless mind,
  my churning heart.

I await the other shoe...
  My poetry darkens.

Foreshadowing.

Ohio

The hills roll slowly in my Ohio home.

The greens, varied,
  the needles of the pines flush.

Even the brightest spring day,
  offering a hint of shadow to all,
    a pleasant disguise,
      a new mystery unfolded at each turn.

The white water rushes along the river,
  breaking at each bend,
    billowing up upon itself at some new
    collision.

Thousands of miles I traveled to don these
new glasses through which I now see my
birthplace.

Scarred,
  I return home,
    dumfounded by the healing beauty that
    surrounds me.

Be Gone

I sit suspended in disbelief of the
happiness that awaited me on the other
side of this road traversed.

Animation moves in contours across my
face;
   laughter bellows from the deepest wells
   of me;
     creativity rekindles;
        my breath deepens.

Victorious, I turn my back on the creature
that enslaved me,
   ever mindful of the speed with which it
   may overtake me still, should I stumble.

Be gone!

Exaltation

The grip of torment's hold evaporates from
the surface of my soul.

Solitude ceases,

  loneliness leaves,

    bitterness' bite beckons no more.

Free,

  I flee from fear's prison.

Bliss is mine,

  ever watchful for misery's pursuit.

Exaltation.

Patience

Acceptance eludes me,

but just for now.

Conscious of my compromise,

yet, holding hope for history's undoing;

I acquiesce to imperfection,

hovering between stringencies and
consolations.

Momentarily,

I pause into life's reality,

yet longingly,

I await harmony's sweet song.

Patience.

Folly

Dreadfully I play the game of mental
Twister,
  jumping from circle to circle,
    the color assignment of my emotional
    turmoil.

The pattern of the playing field
unchanging,
  only the hues of my present path
  fluctuate.

On more stable days,
  I almost feel secure stretching to my
  furthest capability.

Other times,
  the nearest placement seems to elude
  me.

To be the one who spins the game arrow of
my fate is my goal.

Folly.

Blinded

Baffled and confused,
  I await destiny's call,
    feeling unconsulted by fate.

May I have a vote on the path laid out
before me?

Is the road constructed with asphalt,
immovable once set?

Or could I request a highway of gravel,
    still changeable no matter how much
    time passes?

I fear my journey is cast in cement,
  no shaping allowed by my desire.

Confused, I cannot even see the direction
of the road just before me,
  much less its content.

Powerless, I surrender,
  never before so uncertain of my bearing.

Blinded.

Epiphany

Cautiously I ease into the concept of loving
life;
  all things desirable to others reveal
  themselves to me.

The familiar cloak of hopelessness slides
from my shoulders;
  willingness to live life fully,
    so foreign to me,
      inches its way into my spirit.

Is this what others feel daily?

Is this the passion and zeal so taken for
granted by most?

The glass in the window that has always
separated me from them disappears.

Fearful, I cross the threshold into living for
the sake of living.

Hope,
  so unfamiliar,
    covers me like a fine mist.

Epiphany.

Completion

Slowly,

  carefully,

    I sweep the shards of my remaining self
    together.

Tenderly,

  I place them into the receptacle of my
  future self,

    ready for mending.

Merely gathering them as one,

  an effort in and of itself.

Hopefully, I will use what is before me to
assemble the pieces of me,

  making the fragments whole again.

Completion.

Perpetuation

My mother's cloak surrounds me,

    shrouds me from the cold winter of
    home.

Her legacy carries on,

    encircling me and all who surround me
    with her warmth and grace.

Perpetuation.

Distraction

Images of all that did not trespass haunt
my waking hours.

Words spoken and deeper still,
the unspoken.

Sentences written but more intriguing,
the spaces in between.

Here you are before me,
in me,
but not physically present.

Distraction.

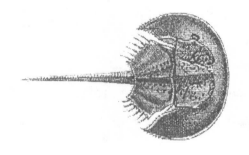

Convolution

Days are all that separate who I am
from who I once was.

Knowledge,
  my burden,
    insight,
      my vice.

The intricacy of the pattern woven by
truth astounds me,
  makes me pause in its complexity.

Love abounds,
  disharmony settles against my skin.

Illusion replaced by the harshness of
reality,
  and the elation of possibility.

Convolution.

Bewilderment

Your touch lingers on the outside of my
clothes,
  the inside of my soul.

The sensation of your flesh pressed
against my lips consumes me.

The roll of your voice in my ear,
  the sound of your heart,
    reaches across the city,
      echoing, echoing, echoing.

Your tone,
  lower,
    reserved only for lovers,
      tickles my neck.

Never have I heard love's sweet melody in
your throat before now.

Never will I be able to shed its
reverberation into my skin,
  my soul.

Still,
  I cannot catch my breath.

My body betrays my will for it.

My spirit remembers you,
  but I know not from where.

Desperately,
  I wish to be free of this, this, ...

I only can hope for escape.

I pray and my answers come one way in
my head,
  yet another in my body.

My physical self carries itself to your door.

I scream at my primal self,
  begging its reason,
    but it knows little discipline.

My arrow's flight is true,
  but it places itself somewhere other than
  my aim.

Bewilderment.

Resurrection

The recent and sudden whirlwind of my
existence slows in its pace;
  the debris of my life begins to settle into
  place.

Out of nothing has arisen the beginning of
my destiny,
  my fate.

The wreckage behind me,
  the stability of simplicity comforts me.

The entrapping of belongings of yesterday,
  only a memory.

In place of the material resides the peace
of minimalism.

What a journey it has been from there to
here.

The physical void that is present blossoms
with the joy of freedom.

Resurrection.

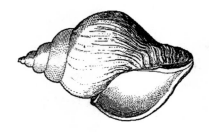

Anticipation

The presence of you moves my spirit,
  strokes my soul,
    and inspires my mind.

Never have I been so clueless as to exactly
who you are to me,
  from whence you came,
    to where you lead.

Yet, never have I been so content to merely
watch the path unfold before me.

Recognition of your role is unnecessary.

The mystery that is you instills passion,
  hope,
    and excitation of the destiny that awaits
    me.

Anticipation.

Serenity

My spirit soars with its newfound freedom;
  the outward blows deflected by my
  conviction.

The comfort of few equates to the approval
of many.

In a heartbeat,
  all changed.
    In a moment,
      I chose self-love.
        In an instant,
          I refused to ever compromise
          myself again.

Stillness becomes me;
  beauty surrounds me;
    love envelops me.

Serenity.

Unity

Finally,

  when I cease seeking you,

    there you are.

When I no longer ask the universe for you,

  you appear.

We meet on mutual ground,

  from the same family,

    the same history,

      the same future,

        perhaps.

Unity.

Deliverance

The deepest parts of my self,
  buried long ago,
    unearthed by you.

The entrance to the tomb of my former self
gives way to your beckoning.

One day,
  I hope all encased beneath will glitter
  with gold,
    embellished by your kiss.

It is you who breaks the seal to the
sarcophagus that holds my purest self.

Deliverance.

Salvation

The seedy rooms,
  crusted with the pain of disease,
    have become home to me.

The podium,
  on its solitary station,
    exudes the presence and wisdom of all
    who have gone before me.

Hope and healing hang in the air with
possibility for all.

Recovery,
  the benefit of so few,
    bodes all,
      yet evades most.

It is with awe and gratitude that I take the
seat that is mine.

As time passes,
  my chronology becomes a rarity.

Such honor bestowed upon me by the
greatest power of all;
  initially, unworthy,
    finally, deserving.

Salvation.

Perfection

What I find beautiful is...

the sculpture of your arm,

the chisel of your cheek,

the arc of your eye,

the sway of your lips,

the lure of your glance.

Perfection.

Dissipation

Peace overtakes me like the predator that
once was my disease,

  the journey from there to here

  so seemingly insurmountable.

The pain,

  the sorrow,

    but mostly the hopelessness that once
was my cloak,

     slips from my shoulders,

      lying in a heap behind me.

Victorious,

  I stand upon the cliff,

   a sentry to my former self.

Dissipation.

Tranquility

The stir in my soul that is you
beckons to me for communion.

Drawn together by forces higher than our
limited human form,
  we unite.

A breath for a breath,
  love encircles us.

A ring for a ring,
  commitment binds us.

At last,
  my turmoil ceases.
    Vitality takes its place.

Passion becomes me,
  joy surround me.

Tranquility.

Liberation

Words spoken,
  once so forbidden,
    now flow from my lips with the ease of
    cascading water.

My voice is found,
  I hide no more.

The rules that once imprisoned me
seem like a tale of sorrow told by another.

Liberation.

Your Adversary

If your adversary,
  whom you once called "friend" died
  tomorrow,
    would you rejoice in your freedom from
    her presence,
      or would you regret the things you
      did,
        the words you said,
          or perhaps more,
            the words you didn't?

Would you celebrate your victory over her,
  finally accomplishing the ultimate
  defeat,
    or would you wonder why it is you
    hated her so to begin with?

If the last words you spoke if not to her,
  but even of her,
    were those of judgment and
    persecution,
      would you be proud?

What is it you would remember her by,

  the kind acts she did for you,

    the supportive words she gave you in a
    painful moment,

      or the defamous character which you,

        and you alone,

          without factual basis or your own
          first hand knowledge,

          used as your sword of
          justification to shun her?

Are you pleased with the kind of person
you were,

  who you showed yourself to be to her
  when last she thought of you?

If what you feel at this moment is pride in
yourself upon this contemplation,

  I applaud you.

If shame presents itself to you,

  even if only as a shadow,

    a glimmer of reality in the periphery of
    your self-observation,

    then I wish you a tomorrow.

Dedication

Our chants of love expressed with
intention,
   never automation.

Kisses exchanged as if the first,
   never in haste.

The embraces full,
   complete,
     not in passing.

Equal depths of emotion shared between
us,
   neither less or more.

Dedication

Precarious

Once again I narrowly escape the death
grip of this disease.

The suddenness with which it can
overtake me tightens the breath in my
chest,
    peril,
      a heartbeat away.

I duck around the corner,
  my back pressed up against the wall of
sanity,
    afraid to look back at the path I just
tread,
      for fear its gravitational pull will
      absorb me.

Darkness surrounds me;
  I look for any path out,
    no matter how dimly lit.

As before,
  the way toward sanity discloses itself.

So many times now,
  too many,
    I dash out of the roar of the avalanche
    of mental demise.

Hiding in the crevice of escape once more,
  all I need do is wait for the tundra to
  pass,
    find the dimly lit path to reprieve.

Still, I fear that the number of escapes is
finite.

Precarious.

Whatever

The chorus of voices singular,
   yet in unison,
     mock me,
       question me,
         and bludgeon me with "if's",
        and "should's",
          and "but for's".

The litany of doubts,
  concerns,
   and fears,
     badger me incessantly.

Round and round they go,
  persistent in their demand for resolution,
   often silenced only by the command of
   my spoken voice -

"Whatever"!

Victory

Hours of our lives spent listening to the
woes of others.

What must total years by now:
  the time given of ourselves,
    sacrificed from kin,
      robbing us our chosen recreations.

To what end?

For what purpose?

The answer thunders from our collective
mouths:
  for service,
    for the joy of offering even just one soul
    the path to salvation,
      and selfishly,
        for our own respite from the fiend,
        alcoholism, that lay in wait for us.

Whether it be dedication to the program
for living so freely offered to us,
  or for our own selfish need to arrest this
  heathen that dogs us,
    we give,
      we share,
        we carry on.

Together we raise our shields in defense of
our enemy,
   not fighting it,
     just protecting ourselves from the
     terminal plague of addiction.

Just as we work to better ourselves,
   our future,
     so our children might have more than
     do we,
       together,
         we sacrifice of ourselves so the
         afflicted who sicken long after we
         have recovered might heal.

We give our life sustaining blood because
without this,
   we meet our demise anyway.

So, it is to this end, we serve.

Victory.

Bliss

Solemnity eases its grip,
  yet remains.

Its pervasiveness trails me,
   even though contentment returns.

It reveals itself in the smile that overtakes
  my mouth,
   but not my eyes.

Perhaps it is merely the price of long life,
  for no life long lived avoids strife.

Possibly,
  my desire to be rid of its dampness is
  futile.

But still,
  I hold hope to one day be completely free
  from its tenacity.

I dream of soaring high enough that the
altitude alone shears somberness from my
spirit.

Bliss.

Resilience

Cheeks turned,
  looks of condemnation,
    jeers uttered under muddled breath,
      graze off of the shroud of dignity that
      surrounds you.

Piercing stares,
  bodies recoiling with our approach,
    and prejudice,
      stream from your skin like water on
      glass,
        present,
          but not penetrating.

I watch you shine with integrity from
within,
  protected from the leers by the armor of
  self-love.

Resilience.

Longevity

The shuffle of your gait

offsets the quickness of your wit.

Your abundance,

   masked by your humility.

Vast knowledge,

   delivered tongue in cheek.

Fortitude and vigilance

cascade in a wake behind you.

Longevity.

Stillness

End of day's light streams
in layers through the trees.

Sounds of nature,
  familiar and unknown,
    sing hymns from the wood.

My breath,
  tense upon my arrival,
    stills with the press of your presence
    into me.

It is here I have always wanted to be.

Stillness.

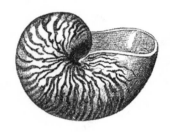

Rejoice

Freedom from the drone that had become
my existence invites me in.

It is there I now dwell with others like-
minded.

They too have moved beyond the sentence
of life and into its thrill.

Rejoice.

Beckoning

Self-satisfaction intertwines with
condemnation of who she is not.

The beauty within masked,
 but only upon her gaze in the mirror.

To all else,
 she is enchanting at first blush.

Her grace,
 only disguised from herself,
  emanates through her,
   from her,
    apparent to all.

Discovery of that which those about her
know innately awaits.

Beckoning.

Clarity

Problems and perils spin in a whirlwind.

Questions posed,
  dilemmas dissected,
    quandaries dancing in unison through
    the states of analysis,
      examined,
        yet, unresolved.

It is not until stillness comes that answers
become audible.

Wisdom's voice is the sound of my own,
  but with a pitch and tenor I have come to
  recognize as originating from a source
  greater than me.

The perpetual vibration that is my inner
turmoil ceases.

In that instance,
  resolution overwhelms me,
    no hesitation,
      no confusion,
        instilled in me by something higher.

Clarity.

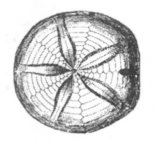

Home

Today we stopped being two and started
being one.

Simplicity entices me.

Predictability's security draws me in,

   the longing for belonging finally
   quenched.

The frenetic climax of our courtship at last
settles into a peaceful pace down life's
corridor.

Home.

Delicacy

The petri dish that is my brain is added to,

subtracted from,

and supplemented by the notions and
tinctures of doctors of varying degrees,

in attempts to bring into perfect
balance the high wire act of my
existence.

Delicacy.

Resolution

Parables,

  analogies,

    and correlations

      sift through the net of contemplation
like so many raindrops on a pane.

Possibilities,

  probabilities,

    and alternate realities

      dance the minuet on stage.

Observations,

  revelations,

    and realizations

      dash through the finish line.

Resolution.

Compassion

Anguish impales me with its familiarity,
  piercing the carefully constructed shelter
  surrounding me.

Fear prepares me for the emotional
tsunami sure to follow,
  experience tells me to rush to defense,
    depression initiates the mantra of
    defeat.

But it is resolution that follows.

Communication replaces degradation,
  compromise,
    more valued than victory;
      love,
        remembered throughout.

Compassion.

Sentiment

The images on film capture the
presentation of us,

  our beauty.

But it is all that is not pictured that is
most intriguing:

  the intensity of our gaze,

    the contours of our smiles in response
    to each other,

    the pervasiveness of our love.

Sentiment.

Perfectionism cannot be applied to that for which there is no standard.

Order Form

To order a copy of Tumultuous Journey, Poems Along the Way, complete the following information and submit your order in the format most convenient for you.

Name:_____

Address:_____

Telephone:_____

Fax:_____

Email:_____

The price is $19.95 plus shipping of $4.25 in the United States for one book and $2.00 for each additional book. For international shipping, add $9.50 for the first book and $6.25 for each additional book.

For orders mailed to addresses in Ohio, please add 6.25% sales tax. All other locations may waive the sales tax charge.

Web: www.invinciblepublishing.ws
Email: orders@invinciblepublishing.ws
Fax: (330) 940-3052
Telephone: (330) 923-8405
U. S. Mail: 1107 North Howard Street
            Akron, Ohio 44310-1331

Printed in the United States
102272LV00003BA/4-9/P